# Table of Contents

# Section I:

# INTRODUCTION

## "Quality and diversity can go hand in hand, and they must."
### — President Bill Clinton

The Federal Government strives to be a model employer by building and maintaining a workforce that reflects the rich diversity of the Nation. Diversity has evolved from sound public policy to a strategic business imperative. It is an issue that requires more attention and support within the Federal workplace, and the U.S. Office of Personnel Management (OPM) is committed to bringing this about. This guide reflects OPM's commitment to diversity and to providing the best possible workplace for all Federal employees.

## Purpose of the Guide

The guide is a tool to help Federal agencies develop an effective program to build and maintain a diverse, high-quality workforce. Building includes activities to attract, recruit, and hire employees. Maintaining includes activities to develop, manage, reward, and retain employees.

The guide is designed to:

- Increase awareness of the business, cultural, demographic, and legal frameworks for understanding and managing diversity.

- Support managers, supervisors, human resource professionals, and other staff in their efforts to respect, appreciate, and value individual differences.

- Increase agencies' understanding of how diverse perspectives can:
  - improve organizational performance,
  - help prevent unlawful discrimination or harassment incidents,
  - improve workplace relations,
  - build more effective work teams,
  - improve organizational problem solving, and
  - improve customer service.

- Identify helpful tools and strategies to obtain, retain, strengthen, and fully utilize a diverse, high-quality workforce.

Equally important, the guide provides agencies a basic blueprint of the actions they can take to build and maintain a diverse, high-quality workforce, which include:
- Positioning the agency
- Designing and implementing a diversity program
- Sustaining commitment

# Section II:

# FRAMEWORKS UNDERPINNING DIVERSITY

Diversity means different things to different agencies, organizations, and people. Federal diversity initiatives have historically focused on equal employment opportunity (EEO) and affirmative employment. The Federal Government must now broaden its view of diversity. It must embrace the business, cultural, and demographic dimensions of diversity as well as the legal dimension. Recognizing the multiple frameworks underpinning diversity is important to shape and pursue the missions and goals of individual agencies and the Federal Government as a whole.

## Business Framework

When the Hudson Institute published Workforce 2000[1] in 1987, the subject of diversity emerged as a topic of national interest. This publication outlined impending demographic changes that would alter the image of the typical American worker. The report predicted that minorities would increasingly constitute a larger percentage of the net new entrants into the workforce. It also noted that the labor force participation of women would continue to rise and that the median age of workers would increase due to the aging baby boom generation. In essence, the American workforce was changing on a par with America's demographics. The Hudson Institute's 1997 follow-up report, Workforce 2020,[2] discussed many of these same trends and affirmed the need to plan proactively for workforce changes.

In its recent report, Futurework: Trends and Challenges for Work in the 21st Century,[3] the U.S. Department of Labor reinforces the Hudson Institute's predictions for a changing workforce. This report states:

"By 2050, the U.S. population is expected to increase by 50 percent and minority groups will make up nearly half of the population. Immigration will account for almost two-thirds of the nation's population growth. The population of older Americans is expected to more than double. One-quarter of all Americans will be of Hispanic origin. Almost one in ten Americans will be of Asian or Pacific Islander descent. And more women and people with disabilities will be on the job."

Clearly, any organizations — including Federal agencies — that want to be successful in today's world must recognize and use diversity to their advantage. Diversity should be an integral part of an agency's business planning and Government Performance and Results Act of 1993 (GPRA) activities.[4] This means that diversity management programs do not stand alone. Instead, they are recognized as being a critical link in achieving the agency's specific mission or business needs, relative to employees, customers, suppliers, and other stakeholders. This is the business case for valuing diversity.

The business case for diversity has two significant elements. First, the labor market has become increasingly competitive. The Federal Government must use every available source of candidates to ensure that each agency has the high-quality workforce that it needs to deliver its mission to the American public. Any agency that fails to take steps to recruit among the full spectrum of the labor market is missing a strategic opportunity.

Second, the changing demographics of America mean that the public served by the Federal Government is also changing. When agencies recruit and retain an inclusive workforce — one that looks like the America it serves — and when individual differences are respected, appreciated, and valued, diversity becomes an organizational strength that contributes to achieving results. Diversity offers a variety of views, approaches, and actions for an agency to use in strategic planning, problem solving, and decision making. It also enables an agency to better serve the taxpayer by reflecting the customers and communities it serves.

This conclusion has been supported by specific research[5] showing that an effective diversity strategy has a positive effect on cost reduction, resource acquisition, creativity, problem solving, and organizational flexibility.    Each of these actions has a direct impact on achieving the mission and business of the agency.

## Cultural Framework

Another important aspect of diversity derives from different cultural perspectives. As an employer, the Federal Government has made great strides in achieving representational diversity. There is, however, still work to do. Misconceptions and misinformation should be replaced by facts, and stereotypes replaced by awareness.

A 1996 U.S. Merit Systems Protection Board (MSPB) study [6] found disparities in the perceptions of minority and White employees with respect to how minority employees are treated in the Federal workplace. Although the MSPB study found no evidence of widespread, pervasive discrimination, it found that minorities and non-minorities have significantly different perceptions about the degree to which discrimination may still be present in the workplace. Further, these differences in perception are so large that they suggest many minority and non-minority employees have great difficulty in understanding or accepting the others' perspective. Some of the significant MSPB findings include:

- Many minority employees believe they are not treated fairly in the Federal civil service. Substantial numbers of minorities report that they are subjected to both blatant and subtle discriminatory practices in the Government's workplace. For instance, 55 percent of Black survey respondents believe that Blacks are subjected to "flagrant or obviously discriminatory practices" in the Federal workplace.

- In contrast, non-minorities generally believed that discrimination is minimal. For instance, only 4 percent of White respondents shared the view of 55 percent of Black respondents that Black employees are subjected to flagrant or obvious discriminatory employment practices. Similarly, only 3 percent of White respondents shared the view of 28 percent of Hispanic respondents that Hispanic employees are subject to flagrant or obvious discriminatory employment practices.

- Overall, minority employees have lower average grade levels than White male employees even after controlling for differences in education, experience or other advancement-related factors.

- On average, minorities receive lower performance ratings and fewer cash awards than Whites in professional and administrative positions.

- Fewer minority employees than White employees receive the developmental opportunities to serve as acting supervisors in the absence of incumbent managers.

The MSPB survey revealed the need for Federal agencies to disseminate accurate data about the exact nature of representation within each Federal agency. This will increase the likelihood that employee perceptions would be based on facts, rather than on misinformation or misconceptions.

A diverse workplace may present other challenges in the area of communication across cultures. For instance, the Federal workplace culture sometimes assigns a specific significance to the workplace behavior of employees (e.g., assuming that sustaining eye contact is a sign of directness and honesty) that may be different from the values in an individual employee's culture (e.g., considering it disrespectful and hostile to sustain eye contact).

# Demographic Framework

The Federal Government has made progress regarding the representation of women and minorities in its workforce. Nevertheless, there is more to do to increase representation of individual minority groups, women, and people with disabilities.

Despite an overall reduction in the total size of the Federal workforce between 1990 and 1998, OPM's Central Personnel Data File (CPDF) data reflect an increase in the representation of minorities (27.6 to 29.4 percent) and of women (42.3 to 42.9 percent). To better understand how the Federal Government is doing, OPM compared these trends to those in the Civilian Labor Force (CLF). In 1990, minorities comprised 21.8 percent of the CLF, rising to 26.4 percent in 1998, while the representation of women went from 45.3 to 46.3 percent.

In 1998, only Hispanics and women remained underrepresented relative to the CLF. Hispanics made up 6.4 percent of the Federal workforce in 1998 versus 10.8 percent of the CLF. Women made up 42.9 percent of the Federal workforce compared to 46.3 percent of the CLF. In addition, the percent of Federal workers that had targeted (severe) disabilities remained at 1.2 percent during the same time period, below the estimated 6 percent availability of Americans with similar types of disabilities who were seeking employment.

Although the above statistics represent aggregate-level snapshots of representation in the entire Federal Government, workforce composition varies considerably by agency. CPDF data show wide differences in the representation of minority groups among executive departments and independent agencies with 500 or more employees.

— Blacks were employed at or above their level of availability in the CLF in 16 of 17 executive departments and all 22 independent agencies.

— Asian/Pacific Islanders were employed at or above their level of availability in the CLF in 14 of 17 executive departments and 12 of 22 independent agencies.

— American Indians were employed at or above their level of availability in the CLF in 14 of 17 executive departments and 12 of 22 independent agencies.

— Hispanics, however, were employed at or above their level of availability in the CLF in only 6 of 17 executive departments and only 5 of 22 independent agencies.

— Similarly, women were employed at or above their level of availability in the CLF in only 7 of 17 executive departments and 10 of 22 independent agencies.

Of the 14,109 senior pay positions (Senior Executive Service, Senior Foreign Service, and others above General Schedule grade 15) in the Federal Government in 1998, 12.1 percent were occupied by minorities (up from 7.7 percent in 1990). Women occupied 21.7 percent of senior pay positions in 1998 (up from 11.1 percent in 1990). In the so called "feeder grades" to senior pay positions, General Schedule grades 13 to 15, minorities comprised 17.4 percent in 1998 compared to 12.7 percent in 1990, while women comprised 27.5 percent in 1998 compared to 18.7 percent in 1997.

# Legal Framework

The United States has passed many laws guaranteeing the rights of citizens to equal protection and due process of law. The landmark legislation outlawing discrimination based on race, color, creed, or national origin is the Civil Rights Act of 1964,[7] as amended. Since then, a number of significant statutes and Executive orders have established the legal foundation for Federal agencies in the areas of EEO and affirmative employment.

Title VII of the Civil Rights Act of 1964, as amended, prohibits discrimination with regard to any personnel action, or a term, condition, or privilege of employment based upon race, color, sex, national origin, or religion. The Civil Rights Act of 1991[8] amended the 1964 law to, among other things, expand the types of damages available in Federal EEO cases for intentional discrimination and to clarify the burden of proof in adverse impact cases. The Pregnancy Discrimination Act of 1978[9] further amended the Civil Rights Act of 1964 to prohibit employment decisions based upon an employee's pregnancy, childbirth, or related medical condition.

Executive Order 11478,[10] issued in 1969, prohibits discrimination in the executive branch of the Federal Government on the basis of race, color, religion, sex, national origin, disabilities, or age. In 1998, the President amended this Executive Order to also prohibit discrimination on the basis of sexual orientation.[11] While these Executive Orders do not create additional enforcement rights, they firmly establish the policy regarding equal employment in the executive branch.

The Rehabilitation Act of 1973,[12] as amended, prohibits discrimination against individuals with disabilities on the basis of their disabling conditions. The Americans with Disabilities Act of 1990 (ADA),[13] which also prohibits discrimination against individuals with disabilities, applies to the Federal Government through the Rehabilitation Act.[14] Drug and alcohol abuse are covered by the Rehabilitation Act as well as the Miscellaneous Provisions Relating to Substance Abuse and Mental Health.[15]

The Age Discrimination in Employment Act (ADEA)[16] provides protection to persons who are age 40 or over. It does not prohibit, however, all discrimination on the basis of age, such as maximum entry level ages for initial appointment as a law enforcement officer.

The passage of the Congressional Accountability Act of 1995[17] extended the Federal protections under Title VII, the Rehabilitation Act, ADA, and ADEA to legislative branch employees.

The Equal Pay Act[18] prohibits discrimination based upon sex in the payment of wages and fringe benefits for equal work in jobs requiring equal skill, effort, and responsibility, and which are performed under similar working conditions. Claims of wage discrimination based upon sex can be brought either under the Equal Pay Act, or Title VII, or both.

In addition to the laws prohibiting discrimination on the basis of race color, sex, national origin, religion, age, or sexual orientation, the Federal Government acts proactively in the area of affirmative employment. Federal agencies report to OPM the results of their Federal Equal Opportunity Recruitment Program (FEORP) activities. FEORP was established under the Civil Service Reform Act of 1978.[19] It requires agencies to maintain equal opportunity recruitment programs for minorities and women. Federal agencies also submit annual reports to the Equal Employment Opportunity Commission (EEOC) regarding their Affirmative Employment Program

(AEP).  The AEP addresses efforts and accomplishments in recruitment, promotions, training, hiring, and other advancement opportunities for women and minorities.[20]  In addition, the Rehabilitation Act of 1973, as amended, also requires Federal agencies to develop Affirmative Action Plans for the hiring, placement, and advancement of people with disabilities.

Three executive branch agencies — EEOC, OPM, and MSPB — have responsibility for establishing, overseeing, and enforcing the civil rights laws and affirmative employment programs.

---

1.  Johnson, W.B. & Packer, A.H.  Workforce 2000: Work and Workers for the 21$^{st}$ Century.  Indianapolis, Indiana: Hudson Institute (1987).

2.  Judy, R.W. & D'Amico, C.  Workforce 2020: Work and Workers in the 21$^{st}$ Century.  Indianapolis, Indiana: Hudson Institute (1997).

3.  U.S. Department of Labor, Futurework: Trends and Challenges for Work in the 21$^{st}$ Century.  Washington, DC. (Labor Day 1999).

4.  Pub. L. 103-62, 107 Stat. 285, (Aug. 3, 1993).

5.  Cox, T., Jr., & Blake, S.  Managing cultural diversity: Implications for organizational competitiveness.  Academy of Management Executive, 5(2), 34-47.

6.  U.S. Merit Systems Protection Board, Fair and Equitable Treatment: A Progress Report on Minority Employment in the Federal Government.  Washington, DC. (1996).

7.  See 42 U.S.C. §§2000e et seq.  See also 29 CFR §1614.

8.  See 42 U.S.C. §§2000e et seq.

9.  Pub. L. No. 95-9555 amends Section 701 of the Civil Rights Act of 1964 by adding paragraph (k).  See also 29 CFR §1604.10(a).

10. See Executive Order 11478, Equal Employment Opportunity in the Federal Government (August 8, 1969).

11. See Executive Order 13087, Further Amendment to Executive Order 11478, Equal Employment Opportunity in the Federal Government (May 28, 1998).

12. See 29 U.S.C. §791 et seq.  See also 29 CFR §1614.203.

13. See 42 U.S.C. §§12101 et seq.

14. See 42 U.S.C. §§12111 et seq. and 42 U.S.C. §§12201–204 and 12210.

15. See 42 U.S.C. 290dd.

16.    See 29 U.S.C. §§621 et seq.  29 U.S.C. §§631a(b) and 633a are the only provisions of this Act that apply to Federal employees.

17.    See 2 U.S.C. §1301 et seq.

18.    Amends the Fair Labor Standards Act as codified at 29 U.S.C. §206(d).  See also 29 CFR §§1620 et seq. and 29 CFR §1614.408.

19.    See 5 U.S.C. §7201.

20.    See 42 U.S.C. § 2000e-16.

# BUILDING AND MAINTAINING A DIVERSE WORKFORCE

Numerous tools and strategies are available to Federal agencies to build and maintain a diverse workforce.  These are best managed in three stages:

- Positioning the agency

- Designing and implementing a diversity program

- Sustaining commitment

## Positioning the Agency

After considering the frameworks described in the previous section, agencies will recognize that a diversity program will assist them in achieving their business and strategic goals.  They may want to jump immediately into designing and implementing a series of new initiatives or a completely new diversity program.  However, the key to successfully building a diverse, high-quality workforce for tomorrow begins with a strong leadership commitment and knowledge of where the agency is today.  Moreover, experience has demonstrated that successful diversity initiatives depend on positioning the agency first.

Positioning the agency has several aspects.  First, ensuring strong commitment to the diversity program is essential.  This includes the critical components of top-level leadership support and the commitment of necessary resources (people and funding) to make new initiatives a reality.  Next, it is important to have a realistic picture of agency readiness to move forward, based both on the current demographics of the agency and on the cultural atmosphere and potential impediments that may exist.  Finally, the information from each of these assessments should be integrated into the existing agency workforce planning models and used to target opportunities for recruitment, hiring, and retention.

With this commitment and information firmly in hand, the agency can be confident that it has positioned itself for success in designing and implementing an effective diversity program. The actions and considerations required to position the agency in this way are described in more detail below.

## Commitment

Commitment is the foundation of a successful effort to build and maintain a diverse, high-quality workforce. This commitment should be clearly stated and communicated from the top leadership to employees at all levels. In addition, agencies need to take action to assure that resources and staff are available for each stage of the program. Commitment can be demonstrated through such actions as:

- Encourage a leadership that creates an environment of inclusion and values differences.

- Clearly assign adequate resources to their diversity activities. An agency could choose to clearly identify resources in its budget to diversity initiatives.

- Ensure that senior managers are directly involved in planning and conducting diversity activities.

- Ensure that employees are an integral part of the agency's efforts to plan and conduct diversity activities.

- Consider training employees in intercultural communication to address differences in communication across cultures.

- Establish Special Emphasis Programs (SEPs) and appoint SEP Managers as management advisors on how to obtain and manage a diverse workforce. SEP Managers can be critical to help agencies establish an effective diversity management program. Agencies can appoint SEP Managers on a full-time, part-time or collateral-duty basis to advise agency management on the creation and retention of a diverse workforce. SEP Managers should be clearly interested in improving the agency's workforce diversity and have the required knowledge, skills, and ability to do the work (knowledge of the organization, its needs, and its culture; sufficient experience and established networks; and familiarity with the issues, concerns, and culture of the underrepresented group). They should also have the confidence of agency management so managers will listen to his/her advice and counsel.

- Train managers and supervisors about their EEO and AEP responsibilities as well as the existing tools to help them carry out their responsibilities in these areas.

- Widely disseminate the agency's FEORP and AEP goals throughout the agency, and encourage managers to conduct targeted recruitment in support of such goals.

## Assessing the Current Situation

Agencies must understand their current demographic situation. This is done by developing a workforce profile, that is, a complete picture of their workforce and how it reflects diversity at all levels, in all key occupations, and in all organizational components.

The annual reports that each agency already prepares are good sources of data about the agency workforce. The FEORP and AEP reports provide useful information about an agency's affirmative employment activities and their workforce data. In addition, OPM conducts governmentwide workforce analyses and disseminates reports summarizing this information. OPM also provides technical advice to agencies to help them analyze their own agency data. OPM's website, www.opm.gov, has information about the statistical profiles of women, individual minority groups, and people with disabilities in the Federal civilian workforce.

## Environmental Assessment

Positioning also includes assessing the agency's readiness to create and support a complete diversity management program. Many agencies already have active programs; others are less well established. To design their programs to their best advantage, agencies should develop a good understanding of their individual strengths and weaknesses.

An agency can gather this information by assessing their employees' views on diversity issues. A useful tool for assessing agency readiness is a survey that documents and measures the agency's strengths and weaknesses in promoting diversity. Variously called a "cultural audit" or "organizational assessment," this survey is an organized method to examine such questions as:
  — What structures are in place to support strong diversity management?
  — What impediments do agency employees see that may affect the design of the program?

— Are agency values present to sustain commitment to the program?

Ideally, the survey will identify strengths and weaknesses in the agency with regard to:
— diversity incorporated into agency vision or mission statement
— diversity statement issued by agency head
— diversity initiative implementation plan
— diversity council/group charter
— diversity policy, directive, administrative order, etc.
— diversity resource center or diversity reading room
— diversity awareness material
— diversity training
— formal mentoring program
— informal mentoring program
— internship program
— awards and incentives
— communications media (e.g., newsletter, intranet)
— accomplishment or status report
— Special Emphasis Program Managers

## Workforce Planning

Analyzing workforce trends and projections, determining skills gaps and needs, and devising succession planning strategies are critical steps for agency strategic and business planning. These activities provide the facts managers need so they know where to assign resources, how to plan for the future work of the organization, and where to focus their energy to produce a high performance organization. This information is used to assess whether the current workforce will assist in meeting tomorrow's goals. It will also help to understand where the recruitment or retention focus should lie and what other actions are needed to create a supportive work environment. Diversity program activities and objectives should be directly integrated into the agency's broader workforce planning activities. For example, workforce planning will surface opportunities for targeted recruitment.

A succession planning program is a deliberate and systematic effort by an agency to ensure continuity of leadership and critical staff skills in mission-critical positions as well as to encourage individual development. Succession planning is a subset of workforce planning, and is designed to ensure the continued effective performance of an agency by identifying, developing, and replacing key people over time. Again, succession planning provides an opportunity to align diversity management programs with the larger agency objectives.

# Designing and Implementing a Diversity Program

When an agency is positioned for success, it can proceed to design and implement its diversity program to include those specific elements that will serve to build and maintain its diverse, high-quality workforce. In particular, the various assessments of the workforce profile, the agency's environment, and future workforce needs should have identified strengths, weaknesses, and targets of opportunity. Those will be important to factor into the specific activities that comprise the diversity program itself.

In general, an agency's diversity program must include elements that build diversity, through recruitment, outreach and hiring, and elements that maintain diversity, through the agency's use of learning and development, rewards and recognition, and a supportive work environment. A successful diversity program needs close, continuing partnerships between human resources and EEO/civil rights and special emphasis staff. In other words, each agency should have in place a comprehensive process to build and maintain a diverse, high-quality workforce.

## Building a Diverse, High-Quality Workforce

Based on the results of assessing the current situation and the environment and conducting workforce planning, an agency will have identified the type and number of positions to be filled as well as any targeted needs. The agency is then ready to design a strategy to find and hire the diverse, high-quality workforce to achieve the agency's mission. To build a diverse workforce, agencies should incorporate tailored approaches to recruit and hire these individuals into their overall strategies. The first step is to find the candidates.

### Recruitment

The purpose of effective recruiting is to attract strong candidates who are prepared both to meet the agency's strategic goals and priorities and to work in the agency's environment. Suggestions for effective recruitment techniques include:

■ Ensure that recruiters and selection officials work closely with human resources and EEO/civil rights/special emphasis staff during the recruiting process. Maintaining close relationships with the experts will facilitate a smooth and easy recruiting process.

■ Know the competition and their recruiting needs. Issuing one vacancy announcement is no longer an effective method of finding candidates. Learn where the candidates go to find jobs and information about finding jobs — make sure the agency's message can be found. Consider using a variety of common job search locations, such as:
— college placement centers,
— minority student associations,
— college organizations of students with disabilities,
— high schools,
— Internet websites,
— newspapers and magazines,
— community newsletters,
— radio announcements,
— community centers,
— professional organizations,
— minority organizations,
— libraries, and
— grocery stores.

In addition, employees can provide recommendations regarding good sources of diverse candidates (their alma maters, professional organizations, etc.).

■ Candidates must feel there is a match between their personal goals and the agency's goals. To create and foster a positive image, state the agency's mission and goals clearly and include an inspiring vision. Develop a theme for the recruiting message and craft it to fit each audience.

■ When developing a recruitment plan, consider campus visits, job fairs, brochures, displays, and website use.

■ Design a long-term recruitment plan with input from managers, supervisors, and employees, as well as from specialists in the areas of human resources management and EEO/civil rights/special emphasis. Be creative.

■ Develop and maintain long-term partnerships with academia and professional associations for the purpose of recruiting high-quality candidates. The goal of partnering is to start the recruitment process ahead of the actual recruitment schedule. Relationships with these sources, which are often best formalized through memoranda of understanding or formal agreements, can afford both sides opportunities for increased awareness and opportunities.

Examples of partnering activities include:
— making regular presentations to faculty, students, and the community about issues of interest to both the agency and the school or community
— making visits to high schools, using video tapes and CD-ROMs to describe the agency's work
— hosting field trips to the agency
— sponsoring agency employee volunteer activities such as mentoring and tutoring
— offering presentations at meetings and conferences of professional associations

- Consider partnering with OPM to help spread information about Federal job opportunities by supporting the installation of touchscreen computers in academic institutions with high enrollments of minorities.

- To help educate the Federal workforce of the future, work closely with minority academic institutions, school systems with significant minority representation, and minority-serving organizations throughout the Nation.

- Design activities to support Executive orders[1] to strengthen the capabilities of minority academic institutions. This will enhance the institutions' ability to provide minorities with the skills and competencies that Federal agencies need.

- Widely publicize job opportunities inside and outside the Federal Government. Agencies now have the ability to develop their own vacancy announcements and instantly post them on USAJOBS network of information systems (Website, telephone, and kiosks) where they can be seen worldwide, 24 hours a day. Agencies should explore ways to recruit from all sources when filling positions, including those in the Senior Executive Service and managerial and supervisory positions at grades GS-13 to GS-15, in order to attract diverse candidates.

- Make sure vacancy announcements provide a realistic preview of the jobs and that they highlight points of interest. Think about what would make an exceptional person want to work for the agency.

- Select a diverse cadre of recruiters that includes representatives from program areas as well as staff areas such as human resources and EEO/civil rights/special emphasis. They should have the ability to deliver the recruiting message effectively. This is an essential step in achieving quality results in recruiting for diversity.

- Ensure that senior managers are directly involved in planning and conducting recruitment activities. As leaders who are familiar with their agency's cultures and needs, as managers who understand skills needs, and as selecting officials, they are an important part of the agency's recruitment activities.

- Design a training program for recruiters that includes information about internal hiring procedures, personnel flexibilities, effective interview techniques, affirmative employment goals, and appropriate questions and behavior.

- Follow up with candidates. Send follow up letters or make phone calls to candidates who were met on the recruitment trips. It is important to make sure that candidates have access to someone knowledgeable after the recruiting contact is over.

## Hiring

After finding high-quality candidates, the agency must now hire them. When implementing a diversity program, several aspects of hiring are important to consider:

- Review internal human resources policies, processes, and operations. Often, if agencies are unable to make quick job offers, good candidates are lost to competitors who are able to move quickly. Many flexibilities are available to agencies and reviewing internal staffing procedures may identify new ways to streamline hiring.

- Take full advantage of customizing the competitive process by using the many staffing flexibilities and hiring authorities available. Take full advantage of technology by using USAJOBS and accepting on-line applications.

- Consider using a variety of available hiring authorities. The best method to fill jobs will differ depending on the situation. Commonly used appointing authorities include:
  - Student Employment Program. The program has two components: Student Temporary Employment and Student Career Experience. Both programs offer valuable, paid work experience to all students — high school, vocational and technical, associate degree, undergraduate and graduate. Students may be employed year-round and receive a flexible schedule of work assignments.

- — Presidential Management Program (PMI) Program. This two-year internship program is designed to attract to the Federal service outstanding graduate students (Master's and Doctoral-level) from a wide variety of academic disciplines who have an interest in, and commitment to, a career in the analysis and management of public policies and programs. Upon successful completion of the internship, PMIs are eligible for conversion to a permanent Government positions and further promotional opportunities

- — Selective Placement Opportunities. These include special appointing authorities for people with disabilities. The use of these authorities provides a unique opportunity for appointees to demonstrate their potential to successfully perform the essential duties of a position.

- ■ Use the Outstanding Scholar and Bilingual/Bicultural hiring authorities as a supplement to competitive examinations to recruit at the GS-5 and GS-7 levels for positions covered by the Luevano consent decree, as appropriate.

- ■ Hire for part-time, intermittent, and seasonal work, or use temporary and term appointments where appropriate. This may attract a group of candidates who are not currently interested in full time or permanent jobs.

- ■ Consider using the authority to pay recruitment and relocation bonuses to increase the agency's ability to compete with other employers.

## Maintaining a Diverse, High-Quality Workforce

Achieving a diverse, high-quality workforce by successfully attracting and hiring the desired employee mix is only the first step. Having made investments to recruit and hire high-quality employees, the agency risks wasting those efforts absent a strong retention strategy. The agency's next objective is to ensure that their valuable employees stay with the agency. That goal is the focus of the second major set of elements to be included in the design and implementation of the agency's diversity program.

These elements can be described as part of a broad model of rewards, which sustain employee commitment. These rewards include support for:
- — a flexible and supportive work environment, including the quality of the supervision and leadership employees receive
- — an emphasis on learning and development

— effective rewards and recognition systems

These aspects of work and working conditions are clearly becoming at least as important to employees' decisions to stay with an organization as their direct pay and benefits levels.  An agency that commits to cultivating these broader rewards will be far better positioned to retain the diverse workforce it builds.

## A Supportive Work Environment

A supportive work environment is one that provides employees with the direction and tools they need to perform the work of the organization to the very best of their ability. As an employer, the Federal Government offers many governmentwide programs to support employees; other aspects of a supportive work environment are in the hands of individual agencies.  Actions to support employees include:

- Ensure that supervisors and managers are provided leadership and diversity training. Their understanding of the benefits and rewards of a diverse workforce helps create a supportive work environment that enhances the potential of all employees.

- Emphasize existing quality of worklife initiatives as effective policies that advance the interests of a diverse workforce.  These initiatives include programs such as:
  — Alternative Work Schedules
  — Family-Friendly Leave Programs
  — Part-time Employment and Job Sharing
  — Telecommuting
  — Dependent Care Support Programs
  — Employee Assistance Programs

- Develop a process to provide reasonable accommodation to job applicants and employees with disabilities.  Agencies are required to make reasonable accommodations to the physical and mental limitations of an applicant or employee who is a qualified person with a disability, unless the accommodation would impose undue hardship on the agency.  In addition, competitive service agencies shall include reasonable accommodation language in job announcements to inform applicants with disabilities that Federal agencies will consider reasonable accommodation requests.

- Ensure that agency facilities offer a safe and productive work environment. Employees spend a significant portion of their lives in agency surroundings.

Keeping them pleasant conveys a sense of pride and respect that helps keep employees on board.

■ Foster a community spirit and a sense of belonging by offering employees a vehicle for becoming involved outside the formal workplace in a variety of recreational and volunteer activities.

## Learning and Development

Professional development and training opportunities are important reasons why valued employees choose to stay with an organization. Agencies can use a variety of approaches to establish a climate that supports continuous learning and development, including:

■ Establish clear paths for acquiring the skills, knowledge, and experience that employees need for their continual learning and career development.

■ Use a variety of ways to provide training and development experiences for employees, such as:
— developing formal and informal mentoring programs,
— using CD-ROMs and other interactive and on-line training technology,
— using internal and external training courses, and
— establishing individual learning accounts (ILAs).

■ Provide training opportunities for all employees. Through investments in training, agencies reflect the value they place on employees and support employees in their own interest in keeping their skills updated in order to remain competitive.

■ Encourage employees to become mentors. In particular, senior managers should be strongly encouraged to mentor individuals from different cultural, racial, or academic backgrounds.

■ Use tuition reimbursement programs. Agencies have the authority to pay all or part of the necessary expenses for training and formal education.

■ Widely publicize developmental opportunities for employees, such as detail assignments and leadership training, to give everyone interested a chance to participate in assignments that prepare them for higher-level positions.

Rewards and Recognition

The systems that reward and engage employees are key to maintaining a diverse, high-quality workforce. All people desire to see their efforts acknowledged. Many aspects of Federal pay, awards, and benefits systems are subject to governmentwide policies and procedures. Nonetheless, agencies must be vigilant about ensuring that merit and results serve as the drivers of differences in rewards. Agencies should use all aspects of pay flexibilities and awards to retain top employees.

- Use awards to recognize significant contributions. These can be lump sum awards or accelerated pay provided through quality step increases. Agencies should continually monitor their use of awards, incentives, and recognition to ensure that individuals and groups all receive their fair share based on transparent criteria and well-understood processes for nominating and granting awards.

- Consider paying retention allowances when challenged to keep particular skills available. Agencies should continually monitor the use of such allowances to check for any evidence of discrimination, and act quickly in the event any is detected. Such internal accountability will help preserve the credibility of such tools and their utility for dealing with retention problems.

# Sustaining Commitment

The mark of a truly successful diversity program is one that becomes ingrained in the culture and the business processes of an agency and is sustained over time. Agencies can take several steps to facilitate this continuity.

## Monitor Results

Agencies should develop systems of measures to continually monitor the effectiveness of their diversity initiatives and make adjustments as needed. The results should be shared and discussed with senior managers and supervisors.

- Regularly monitor the agency workforce profile. Periodic analysis of the resulting data will help determine progress and successes. In turn, the data may be used to adjust recruiting strategies and other workforce planning initiatives as needed.

- Monitor existing career development systems and programs (e.g., who is being chosen for non-routine assignments, special projects, rotational opportunities, training, and conference participation) to ensure that cultural bias is not a factor in participation rates. Evaluate and re-engineer career development systems and programs to better achieve the agency's diversity goals.

- Work with EEO/civil rights office to monitor agencywide numbers and trends regarding formal EEO complaints.

- Monitor the number and diversity of applicants and participants in developmental opportunities and assess the effectiveness of the publicity efforts.

## Accountability

To succeed in developing and sustaining strong diversity initiatives, agency heads should hold their executives, managers, and supervisors accountable for achieving results. OPM also assesses agencies' effectiveness in implementing diversity initiatives.

- Build accountability for hiring, retaining, and developing a diverse, high-quality workforce into the performance management systems for managers and supervisors.

- Ensure that candidates for the Senior Executive Service have certain leadership competencies which include "Cultural Awareness." Selecting officials are accountable for ensuring that the candidates provide examples which evidence possession of such competencies.

## Celebrate Success

In addition to holding managers and supervisors accountable for building and maintaining a diverse, high-quality workforce, agencies should also remember to recognize successes.

- Identify and reward champions, publicizing their accomplishments.

- Consider nominating senior executives for Presidential Rank Awards to recognize their accomplishments related to building and maintaining a diverse, high-quality workforce. The Rank Award is the highest level of recognition a member of the

Senior Executive Service can receive. The selection criteria for this award use ECQs to recognize executives who have demonstrated unusual success in building and maintaining a workforce that is diverse, well trained, highly motivated, and productive.

- Consider establishing an agencywide diversity award.

## OPM Leadership Activities

OPM is assessing agencies' effectiveness in implementing their diversity initiatives.

— OPM's Office of Merit Systems Oversight and Effectiveness reviews agency efforts and results as part of its overall assessment of the effectiveness of personnel management in each agency. Individual oversight reports to each agency includes the findings regarding diversity issues.

— OPM reviews and reports on the progress of each agency's Hispanic Employment Initiative in its "Annual Report to Congress: Federal Equal Opportunity Recruitment Program."

OPM ensures that the Federal Government's senior executives are selected and developed for leadership competencies that support diversity. These leadership competencies are associated with the Executive Core Qualifications (ECQs), which are the foundation upon which senior executives are selected and developed governmentwide. "Cultural Awareness" is the ability to initiate and manage cultural change within the organization to impact organizational effectiveness. The key characteristics are:

— "Valuing cultural diversity and other differences; fostering an environment in which people who are culturally diverse can work together cooperatively in achieving organizational goals."

— "Assessing employees' unique developmental needs and providing developmental opportunities that maximize employees" capabilities and contribute to the achievement of organizational goals; developing leadership in others through coaching and mentoring."

— "Resolving conflicts in a positive and constructive manner. This includes promoting labor/management partnerships and dealing effectively with employees relations matters, attending to morale and organizational climate issues, handling administrative, labor management, and EEO issues, and taking disciplinary actions when other means have not been successful."

## Continuing Communication and Development

To sustain the successes of expanding the diversity of the workforce, agencies should ensure that they have effective communications strategies and diversity training in place for managers, supervisors, and employees.

— Provide training to all staff and managers about practical ways to make a diverse workforce a strength for the entire organization. This may include such subjects as the value of understanding differences, identifying an agency's culture and values, and cross-cultural communication.

— Train managers and supervisors about their EEO and AEP responsibilities as well as the existing tools to help them carry out their responsibilities in these areas.

▪ Sponsor special observances to help educate the general workforce about the contributions of diverse groups and/or help eliminate some of the stereotypes that serve as impediments to full employment. The SEP Managers can help plan and implement these events.

---

**OPM Leadership Activities**

OPM's management leadership curriculum is keeping pace with the evolution of diversity. In these key leadership seminars, managers and executives learn how to make diversity an organizational advantage. The Management Development Centers offer a diversity seminar, "Diversity: A Business Necessity for the Millennium," for individuals GS-13 through GS-15 or equivalent who have responsibility for supervising or managing a workforce and who want a better understanding of how to build and manage a diverse, high-quality workforce. The seminar focuses on how to treat diversity as an important organizational advantage for public organizations of the 21st century. OPM has also incorporated the subject of diversity into the Federal Executive Institute's offerings to members of the Federal Senior Executive Service.

---

---

1. See Executive Order 12900, Educational Excellence for Hispanic Americans (February 22, 1994); Executive Order 12876, Historically Black Colleges and Universities (November 1, 1993); Executive Order 13021, Tribal Colleges and Universities (October 19, 1996); and Executive Order 13125, Increasing Participation of Asian Americans and Pacific Islanders in Federal Programs (June 7, 1999).

# Section IV:

# CONCLUSION

As the employer of a diverse workforce, the Federal Government has come a long way, but still has more work to do. Federal agencies have an opportunity to demonstrate their commitment to having the best workforce possible — one that is diverse and of high quality — to conduct the Nation's business.

This guide provides information and ideas on strategies and activities to build and maintain such a workforce. However, there are many Federal agencies that have already developed innovative strategies and activities and are deriving positive results from them. Many Federal agencies are conducting diversity audits, establishing partnerships with academic institutions serving minority populations, creating innovative recruitment programs, setting up clear accountability measures, and designing and providing effective training.

OPM encourages agencies to share their experiences and lessons learned because they can serve as models for the rest of the Federal Government. OPM will add this information to the electronic version of this guide on OPM's website, www.opm.gov. OPM also welcomes comments, suggestions, and ideas on building and maintaining a diverse, high-quality workforce.

www.ingramcontent.com/pod-product-compliance
Lightning Source LLC
Chambersburg PA
CBHW081414170526

45166CB00010B/3345